In Memory of

GRACE FLOOD

THE GRANDMA MOSES OF ARCHBALD

© DEMCO, INC. 1990 PRINTED IN U.S.A.

LACKAWANNA COUNTY
LIBRARY SYSTEM
PENNSYLVANIA

DEMCO

4-29-98

First published in October 1992.
Created and produced for Ediciones B, S.A.
by o3 BCN Packagers.
Text: Albert Delmar
Translation: M. Ellen Oliver
Illustrations: F. Salvà

© 1992, Ediciones B, S.A.
Rocafort, 104   08015 Barcelona (Spain)

ISBN: 84 - 406 - 3121 - 9
Depósito legal: CO 1026 - 1992
Printed and bound in Spain

Cover:
Joan Miró

U.S. & Canada Sole Importer/ Distributor
Trans-National Trade Development Corporation
New York City
Toll Free: (800) 592-2209
Telephone: (212) 922-0450
Fax: (212) 922-0462

Printed by Graficromo, S.A.
Córdoba (Spain)

MIRÓ

The ant and the stars

6

The story of Joan Miró

"I find all of my subjects in the country and at the beach. Pieces of anchor, starfish, pieces of rudder - all of these things appear in my compositions, in the same way that the whimsical mushroom heads and the seventy-seven pumpkin shapes do". (Joan Miró)

Here Joan Miró is talking about Mont-roig, a small village near Tarragona, on the Mediterranean coast of Spain.

The landscape of Mont-roig was so important to him that many times it has been written that he was born there. Actually, Joan Miró, son of a family of craftsmen, was born in the heart of Barcelona.

Even as a child, Miró wanted to be a painter, but at first his parents did not take his ambitions seriously and they sent him off to study commerce. At the same time, he attended classes at an art school where the professors were a bit old-fashioned. For Miró the student, it was difficult to make his drawings realistic. His teachers did not like his work at all, and he failed all the exams.

Then his parents forced him to leave the art school and they put him to work as a clerk in a wholesale company.

Closed up in the office all day, among numbers and papers, Miró became sad, so much so that he even became seriously ill.

His parents, worried about his health, sent him to the country, to Mont-roig, to get better.

Submerged in that beautiful landscape, Miró regained his joy, his health and, above all, his great urge to paint.

When he returned to Barcelona, he was already totally dedicated to painting. At that time, Paris, the capital of France, was the gathering point for the most advanced and daring artists. Picasso, Dufy, Breton... Many of them were friends and lived near each other.

Miró wanted to meet them. When he was 22 he enthusiastically prepared his first trip there. Shortly before leaving, he wrote a letter. It only contained three words: "PARIS, PARIS, PARIS".

Miró's first exhibitions were a failure. Almost no one liked his paintings; his art was not understood. He had a very difficult time in Paris. He painted and painted, hardly ever leaving his studio; but he could not sell a single painting and he did not even have enough money to eat.

In 1928, at the age of 35, he held a very important exposition in which all of the paintings were sold.

The constant and persistent effort of all those years began to bear its first fruit. Great experts began to take notice of him and to appreciate his art. From then on, exhibitions of his work were organized in cities around the world and soon he was considered a brilliant artist.

The Masia

"I think it is foolish to give more value to a mountain than to an ant, and that is why I do not hesitate to spend hours and hours bringing an ant to life." (Joan Miró)

A masia is a typical country house in Catalonia, isolated and surrounded by farmland. It is made of stone, with two or three floors and a double sloping roof.

The ground floor is usually used as stables and for storing farm tools and machinery.The second floor is the house and the third floor is used as an attic or barn.

A cypress tree is commonly found in the front yard - it is a traditional sign of welcome.

The owners of the farm usually lived in the masia. Nowadays, the majority of masias are no longer used as farmhouses.

The Masia (1922)
Oil on canvas, 52,8x58,8 inches
Mrs. Hemingway collection, New York

In this picture Miró painted every detail of a place dear to him: the masia in Mont-roig, where he spent so much time.

Joan Miró worked on this picture for nine months, painting seven or eight hours a day.

Once it was finished, he took it to Paris, where he tried to sell it. But no one was interested in it. One gallery owner named Rosenberg, even proposed selling it in small pieces.

One day, however, a group of well-known people went to visit Miró at his studio in Paris. They saw the painting and they liked it. One of them bought it for a good sum of money - it was Ernest Hemingway, the famous novelist who wrote *The Old Man and the Sea*. This writer was a war correspondent in Spain in 1937. During his stay in Spain he wrote articles for various United States newspapers, in addition to the novel *For Whom The Bell Tolls*.

There are so many things in this picture! Nothing is missing: the people working, the tools, the wagon...

The animals who help the farmers in their work are resting in the shade of the stable.

Meanwhile, a small lizard is calmly basking in the sun.

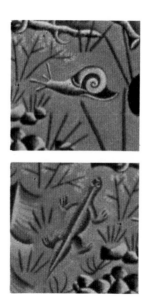

And there are many other details: the rooster and hens, some rabbits, a big tree painted leaf by leaf, the vegetable garden, the pail and watering can, a frog jumping, the duck's tracks...

Dutch interior I

In 1928 Miró took a trip to Holland, where he saw many pictures.
When he returned, he brought reproductions of the ones he had liked best. Later, he would paint some of them in his own style.

   This is Miró's interpretation of the picture *The lute player* by the realist painter H. M. Sorgh.
   At first glance, we do not understand anything.
   A room full of creatures and fantastic, magic objects, as if out of a dream… We begin to discover them quickly. Let your imagination run free!

Dutch interior I (1928)
Oil on canvas, 36,8x29,2 inches
Museum of Modern Art, New York

Near the ceiling, next to the star, a bird flies. From the window we can see a fantastic landscape.

18

A lute player, crazy about music, sings enthusiastically. His
moustache is located a bit far from his mouth and his nose.

Watch out - a vampire is coming! Besides him, there are lots of other strange creatures roaming around the room.

But the dog does not flinch. He stays sitting in his corner and thinks "Where could the cat be?" Can you help him find it?

21

Dawn

Joan Miró painted this picture when he was 75. How simple it seems! It is an abstract picture - the shapes no longer imitate reality. But if we let our imagination run free, we can see many things.

Throughout the last years of his life, and up to his death in 1983, Joan Miró continued to work in the bright studio that the Catalan architect Josep Lluís Sert had designed for him.

This same architect also created the building of the Miró Foundation in Barcelona, which houses an important collection of works donated by the artist.

Dawn (1968)
Oil on canvas, 64,8x52 inches
Pierre Matisse Gallery, Nueva York

Just by reading the title - *Dawn*, we already have a clue. Now let's look at the picture and, guided by its apparent simplicity, we begin to read the signs.

Besides the black, there are only four colors - the colors of the earth and the sky, the sun and the stars.

Red, blue, green, yellow... colors of the landscape of Mont-roig - colors of Miró.

We can see a star, and we can see a bird. Can you see the shape of a woman?

Joan Miró never tired of working and investigating. He always looked for new means to express his own particular way of feeling shapes and colors.

He worked with all types of paints on the most incredible materials, such as sack fabric or newspaper...

He also used his own unique means of expression to create hundreds of sculptures and ceramic objects (in collaboration with his friend J. Llorens Artigas), engravings, murals, tapestries, theater sets and costumes...

Despite the force and energy his work emanates, Miró was a simple man with a calm appearance. He lived a fairly tranquil life and never liked to be treated as a genius or a master. He preferred to be considered simply a worker in art.

A street in Prades (1917)
Oil on canvas
Mrs. Pilar Juncosa collection.

Self-portrait (1919)
Oil on canvas, 30x24 inches
Picasso Museum, Paris.

The table or Still life with rabbit (1920)
Oil on canvas, 52x44 inches
Gustav Zumsteg collection, Zurich.

28

Joan Miró

1893 Born in Barcelona on April 20th.

1907 He begins his studies at the School of Commerce of Barcelona, and frequents the School of Fine Arts of the Lonja.

1911 Upon falling ill, he spends a long convalescence at the family's masia in Mont-roig (Tarragona), where he concentrates on painting.

1912 He exhibits for the first time at the Galerías Dalmau in Barcelona. Some landscapes and still lifes are from this period: *Ciurana*, *The card players of Mont-roig*, *The coffee mill*, and portraits of *Cassany*, *Sunyer*, *Ráfols* and *Ricart*, as well as a self-portrait.

1919 His first trip to Paris, where he meets Picasso and contacts with the Dadá group.

1920 He paints *The table* and begins *The masia*.

1921 His first exhibition at the Galerie La Licorne in Paris.

1924 He becomes good friends with Breton, Éluard and Aragón and signs the first Surrealist Manifesto. *Tilled earth*, *The farm*, *Pastoral* and the *Portrait of Madame K.* are from this period.

1926 He collaborates with Max Ernst on the sets for *Romeo et Juliet* by Diaghilev's Ballets Russes.

1928 He exhibits for the third time in Paris, selling all of the 41 paintings shown and achieving international recognition.

1930 He begins to work on object-sculptures.

1932 He creates the sets, curtain and costumes for *Jeux d'Enfants* by the Ballets Russes of Montecarlo.

1933 He does his first etchings.

1937 He experiments with different materials. He paints *The Catalan harvester* for the Spanish Republic's pavilion at the Universal Exposition in Paris.

1939 The Second World War surprises him in Paris and he moves to Varengeville (Normandy), where he creates his *Constellations*.

Three women (1935)
Oil on cardboard, 42,4x30 inches
Mr. Calder Collection .

Woman and bird at sunrise (1946)
Oil on canvas, 21,6x26 inches
Miró Foundation, Barcelona.

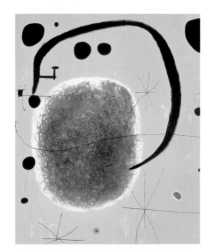

The gold of blue (1967)
Oil on canvas, 82x69 inches
Miró Foundation, Barcelona.

1941 The Museum of Modern Art in New York organizes a retrospective exhibition of Miró's work.

1944 Miró's personal friend Joan Prats publishes the 50 black lithographs of the *Barcelona series.*

1947 He decorates the Terrace Plaza Hotel in Cincinnati.

1948 He exhibits a collection of ceramics created with the collaboration of J. Llorens Artigas at the Galerie Maeght in Paris.

1956 He moves to the island of Mallorca. He exhibits 386 ceramic pieces created with the collaboration of Llorens Artigas at the Galerie Maeght in Paris and the Pierre Matisse Gallery in New York.

1958 Miró and Llorens Artigas make the two famous murals for the UNESCO in Paris: *Sun wall* and *Moon wall.*

1960 Miró creates a ceramic mural for Harvard University.

1962 Beginning in this year, there are various anthological expositions of Miró throughout the world: Paris, Barcelona, London, Zurich, Tokyo...

1975 Fruit of a generous donation on the part of Miró himself, the Miró Foundation, designed by Josep Lluis Sert, is inaugurated.

1977 In collaboration with Josep Royo, he creates a monumental tapestry for the National Art Gallery in Washington, D.C.

1983 Joan Miró dies at the age of 90 in Mallorca.

Joan Miró's works are principally located in:
Miró Foundation, Barcelona, Spain
S.R. Guggenheim Museum, New York, New York, U.S.A.
Museum of Modern Art, New York, New York, U.S.A.
Musée National d'Art Moderne. Centre George Pompidou, París, France.

29

30